POOLS AND RIPPLES

Bliss Perry

POOLS AND RIPPLES

FISHING ESSAYS

By

BLISS PERRY

BOSTON

LITTLE, BROWN, AND COMPANY

1936

DEDICATION

To the friends
who have fished with me
on many a brook and lake and river
of the North Country
especially the Lamoille and the Magalloway
the Margaree, the Marteau Lakes
and the Miramichi

CONTENTS

THE AUTHOR'S APOLOGY

FIRST of all, may the author be forgiven for allowing a photograph of himself to be used as the frontispiece of this book! The irony of the situation lies in his inveterate prejudice against fishermen who stop to pose for their picture when they might at least be trying to land another fish. But in this instance the author had not the remotest idea that he was being snapped by the camera of a fellow fisherman, his attention being fully occupied in striking a land-locked salmon that had strayed down from Parmachenee Lake into the Big Magalloway. The salmon proved to be a small one, but he took the fly in such a royal fashion that his captor was for the moment oblivious of everything else in this world. Hence comes whatever virtue there may be found in the photograph.

The first essay in this collection, "Fishing with a Worm," is reprinted by the courteous permission of the Houghton

Mifflin Company from a volume of essays entitled *The Amateur Spirit*. The essay had already appeared in the *Atlantic* for May 1904, and was published later in that year as a tiny booklet, which has survived several printings. The first issue of this booklet, with a white jacket bearing the motto, "O ye Whales, bless ye the Lord: praise him, and magnify him for ever!" is now prized, I am told, by collectors of angling books. I have even been assured by some enthusiastic brothers of the angle that "Fishing with a Worm" is a classic — but I fear that their notion of a classic is a short treatise, bearing a well-known title, and very rarely read.

"Fishing with a Fly" was first printed in the *Atlantic* in May 1925. It may have been marked by many lapses from good taste, but of two of these, at least, I was soon made acutely conscious. I had referred, most inconsiderately, to an Italian fisherman in Cape Breton as a "bootlegger" and a "Dago." The first epithet was inexact, and the second was ill-chosen. Signor

M., as he promptly informed me, — and I take his word with pleasure, — is not a bootlegger at all, but a wine merchant. For the unfortunate word, "Dago," which I thought I was using affectionately and not in any derogatory sense, I have now substituted "countryman of Saint Francis, Savonarola, and Mussolini." No briefer phrase than that can express my admiration for Signor M.'s skill with the rod; and I am sorry that I ever hurt his feelings.

The other mistake made in that essay — and it still stands uncorrected — was to describe a man whose name I did not know, fishing a river whose name I did not mention, as "the worst fisherman in the world." I straightway received a very sharp letter from a gentleman who thought that he was the person described. He may have been, for it is hard to believe that there are two of that kind. Yet I have very recently been assured that the habitual salmon fishers on a certain river are now divided into two camps, one believing that X. and the other as stoutly maintaining that Y. was the man whom "the magazine fellow" had in mind. I hereby apologize to both X. and Y., though I am confident that I never saw one of them and may never have seen the other. It looks as if there were more claimants to the title of "the worst fisherman in the world" than I innocently supposed was possible.

For still another passage in "Fishing with a Fly" I do not apologize, although it seems that I gave offense to some expert naturalists. They protested vigorously against the assertion that "the man with a rod or gun sees more and feels more in the woods than if he were to go empty-handed." That still seems to me to be a clear sentence and a truism, but many impassioned nature lovers apparently interpreted it as implying that the man with a rod or gun sees more and feels more in the woods than *they*, the naturalists, do! I had no intention of comparing one man's sense perceptions and emotions with those of another. The psychological problems involved are far too complicated for the amateur. Yet I am sure that most lovers of rod and gun will testify that their senses are less alive on those empty-handed days when they are simply strolling through the woods than on the days when eyes and fingers are coördinated and alert. Probably we are all only half awake, at best; and that may explain why we are so quarrelsome.

Perhaps the lesson to be drawn from such controversial correspondence is the very simple one that a writer on angling had better stick to fish, and let men alone. For a fish is universally admitted to be a cold-blooded creature. He has few sensibilities to be outraged. If you merely prick him, he does not bleed. If you tickle him, he will not laugh. A self-respecting trout may indeed feel something like humiliation when he has been hooked on one of those queer flies that you see every spring in the windows of the department stores; but at least the trout refuses to discuss his predicament. A trout's elation on being released from the hook and allowed to go his own way again is often expressed by a

wiggle of the tail which would certainly
indicate gratitude if the trout were a dog.
But, in general, fish may be distinguished
from both dogs and men by their indis-
position to talk back. I hold that this gives
them a high rank in the animal kingdom.

Upon rereading the final essay in this
volume, "Revisiting a River," I feel that
in praising Dr. "C.E.B.C.'s" mastery of the
theory of angling I may have failed to do
justice to his prowess as an actual fisherman. No one who has ever fished with
him has any misgivings on this point; but
to those lovers of the river who prefer
genuine to fictitious exploits I commend an
article entitled "Miramichi Days," written
by the late Professor George B. Churchill
of Amherst, and printed in *Field and Stream*
for August 1924. There is the full story of
the Doctor's resourcefulness in handling a
seventeen-pound salmon on a five-ounce
rod with only twenty-five yards of trout
line and a very light dry-fly leader. This
is thought to be the first salmon killed with
a dry fly on the Miramichi, and surely if

any salmon ever felt honored in yielding to a worthy foe, this one should have saluted C. E. B. C. with a complimentary dying speech. But alas, though a salmon can fight as superbly as Cyrano de Bergerac, he is incapable of romantic declamation. He simply fights till he can fight no longer, and then begins slowly to list and roll over like a torpedoed battleship — and the end comes silently. It is we who should stand at salute.

B. P.

FISHING WITH A WORM

FISHING WITH A WORM

"THE last fish I caught was with a worm."—IZAAK WALTON

A DEFECTIVE logic is the born fisherman's
portion. He is a pattern of inconsistency.
He does the things which he ought not to do,
and he leaves undone the things which other
people think he ought to do. He observes
the wind when he should be sowing, and he
regards the clouds, with temptation tugging
familiarly at his heartstrings, when he might
be grasping the useful sickle. It is a wonder
that there is so much health in him. A
sorrowing political economist remarked to
me in early boyhood, as a jolly red-bearded
neighbor, followed by an abnormally fat
dog, sauntered past us for his nooning:
"That man is the best carpenter in town,
but he will leave the most important job
whenever he wants to go fishing." I stared
at the sinful carpenter, who swung along
leisurely in the May sunshine, keeping
just ahead of his dog. To leave one's job
in order to go fishing! How illogical!

[3]

Years bring the reconciling mind. The world grows big enough to include within its scheme both the instructive political economist and the truant mechanic. But that trick of truly logical behavior seems harder to the man than to the child. For example, I climbed up to my den under the eaves last night — a sour, black sea-fog lying all about, and the December sleet crackling against the windowpanes — in order to varnish a certain fly rod. Now rods ought to be put in order in September, when the fishing closes, or else in April, when it opens. To varnish a rod in December proves that one possesses either a dilatory or a childishly anticipatory mind. But before uncorking the varnish bottle, it occurred to me to examine a dog-eared, water-stained fly book, to guard against the ravages of possible moths. This interlude proved fatal to the varnishing. A half hour went happily by in rearranging the flies. Then, with a fisherman's lack of sequence, as I picked out here and there a plain snell-hook from the gaudy feathered ones, I said to myself with a generous glow at the heart: "Fly-fishing has had enough sacred poets celebrating it already. Is n't there a good deal to be said, after all, for fishing with a worm?"

Could there be a more illogical proceeding? And here follows the treatise, — a Defense of Results, an Apology for Opportunism, — conceived in agreeable procrastination, devoted to the praise of the inconsequential angleworm, and dedicated to a childish memory of a whistling carpenter and his fat dog.

I

Let us face the worst at the very beginning. It shall be a shameless example of fishing under conditions that make the fly a mockery. Take the Taylor Brook, "between the roads," on the headwaters of the Lamoille. The place is a jungle. The swamp maples and cedars were felled a generation ago, and the tops were trimmed into the brook. The alders and moosewood are higher than your head; on every tiny knoll the fir balsams have gained a footing, and creep down, impenetrable, to the edge of the water. In the open spaces the Joe-Pye weed swarms. In two minutes after leaving the upper road you have scared a mink or a rabbit, and you have probably lost the brook. Listen! It is only a gurgle here, droning along, smooth and dark, under the tangle of cedar tops and the shadow of the balsams. Follow the sound cautiously. There, beyond the Joe-Pye weed, and be-tween the stump and the cedar top, is a hand's-breadth of black water. Fly-casting is impossible in this maze of dead and living branches. Shorten your line to two feet, or even less, bait your hook with a worm, and drop it gingerly into that gurgling crevice of water. Before it has sunk six inches, if there is not one of those black-backed, orange-bellied, Taylor Brook trout fighting with it, something is wrong with your worm or with you. For the trout are always there, sheltered by the brushwood that makes this half mile of fishing "not worth while."

Below the lower road the Taylor Brook becomes uncertain water. For half a mile it yields only fingerlings, for no explainable reason; then there are two miles of clean fishing through the deep woods, where the branches are so high that you can cast a fly again if you like, and there are long pools, where now and then a heavy fish will rise; then comes a final half mile through the alders, where you must wade, knee to waist deep, before you come to the bridge and the river. Glorious fishing is sometimes to be had here, especially if you work down the gorge at twilight, casting a white miller until it is too dark to see. But alas, there is a well-worn path along the brook, and often enough there are the very footprints of the fellow ahead of you, signs as disheartening to the fisherman as ever were the footprints on the sand to Robinson Crusoe.

But "between the roads" it is "too much trouble to fish"; and there lies the salvation of the humble fisherman who disdains not to use the crawling worm, nor, for that matter, to crawl himself, if need be, in order to sneak under the boughs of some over-hanging cedar that casts a perpetual shadow upon the sleepy brook. Lying here at full length, with no elbow room to manage the rod, you must occasionally even unjoint your tip and fish with that, using but a dozen inches of line, and not letting so much as your eyebrows show above the bank. Is it a becoming attitude for a middle-aged citizen of the world? That depends upon how the fish are biting. Holing a putt looks rather ridiculous also, to the mere observer, but it requires, like brook fishing with a tip only, a very delicate wrist, perfect tactile sense, and a fine disregard of appearances.

There are some fishermen who always fish as if they were being photographed. The Taylor Brook "between the roads" is not for them. To fish it at all is back-breaking, trouser-tearing work; to see it thoroughly fished is to learn new lessons in the art of angling.

To watch R., for example, steadily filling his six-pound creel from that unlikely stream is like watching Sargent paint a portrait. R. weighs two hundred and ten. Twenty years ago he was a famous amateur

pitcher, and among his present avocations
are violin playing, which is good for the
wrist, taxidermy, which is good for the eye,
and shooting woodcock, which before the
days of the new Nature Study used to be
thought good for the whole man. R. began
as a fly-fisherman, but by dint of passing his
summers near brooks where fly-fishing is
impossible, he has become a stout-hearted
apologist for the worm. His apparatus is
most singular. It consists of a very long,
cheap rod, stout enough to smash through
bushes, and with the stiffest tip obtainable.
The lower end of the butt, below the reel, fits
into the socket of a huge extra butt of
bamboo, which R. carries unconcernedly.
To reach a distant hole, or to fish the lower
end of a ripple, R. simply locks his reel,
slips on the extra butt, and there is a four-
teen-foot rod ready for action. He fishes
with a line unbelievably short, and a Kendal
hook far too big; and when a trout jumps for
that hook, R. wastes no time in manœuv-
ring for position. The unlucky fish is simply
"derricked" — to borrow a word from

Theodore, most saturnine and profane of Moosehead guides.

"Shall I play him awhile?" shouted an excited sportsman to Theodore, after hooking his first big trout.

"—— no!" growled Theodore in disgust. "Just derrick him right into the canoe!" An heroic method, surely; though it once cost me the best squaretail I ever hooked, for Theodore had forgotten the landing net, and the gut broke in his fingers as he tried to swing the fish aboard. But with these lively quarter-pounders of the Taylor Brook, derricking is a safer procedure. Indeed, I have sat dejectedly on the far end of a log, after fishing the hole under it in vain, and seen the mighty R. wade downstream close behind me, adjust that comical extra butt, and jerk a couple of half-pound trout from under the very log on which I was sitting. His device on this occasion, as I well remember, was to pass his hook but once through the middle of a big worm, let the worm sink to the bottom and crawl along it at his leisure. The trout could not resist.

Once, and once only, have I come near equaling R.'s record, and the way he beat me then is the justification for a whole philosophy of worm-fishing. We were on this very Taylor Brook, and at five in the afternoon both baskets were two thirds full. By count I had just one more fish than he. It was raining hard.

"You fish down through the alders," said R. magnanimously. "I 'll cut across and wait for you at the sawmill. I don't want to get any wetter, on account of my rheumatism."

This was rather barefaced kindness — for whose rheumatism was ever the worse for another hour's fishing? But I weakly accepted it. I coveted three or four good trout to top off with — that was all. So I tied on a couple of flies and began to fish the alders, wading waist-deep in the rapidly rising water, down the long green tunnel under the curving boughs. The brook fairly smoked with the rain, by this time, but when did one fail to get at least three or four trout out of this best half mile of the lower brook? Yet I had no luck. I tried one fly after another, and then, as a forlorn hope, — though it sometimes has a magic of its own, — I combined a brown hackle for the tail fly with a twisting worm on the dropper. Not a rise!

I thought of R. sitting patiently in the sawmill, and I fished more conscientiously than ever.

> Venture as warily, use the same skill,
> Do your best, whether winning or losing it,
> If you choose to play! — is my principle.

Even those lines, which by some subtle telepathy of the trout brook murmur themselves over and over to me in the waning hours of an unlucky day, brought now no consolation. There was simply not one fish to be had, to any fly in the book, out of that long, drenching, darkening tunnel. At last I climbed out of the brook, by the bridge. R. was sitting on the fence, his neck and ears carefully turtled under his coat collar, the smoke rising and the rain dripping from the inverted bowl of his pipe. He did not seem to be worrying about his rheumatism.

"What luck?" he asked.

"None at all," I answered morosely. "Sorry to keep you waiting."

"That's all right," remarked R. "What do you think I've been doing? I've been fishing out of the sawmill window just to kill time. There was a patch of floating sawdust there, — kind of unlikely place for trout, anyway, — but I thought I'd put on a worm and let him crawl around a little." He opened his creel as he spoke.

"But I did n't look for a pair of 'em," he added. And there, on top of his smaller fish, were as pretty a pair of three-quarter-pound brook trout as were ever basketed.

"I'm afraid you got pretty wet," said R. kindly.

"I don't mind that," I replied. And I did n't. What I minded was the thought of an hour's vain wading in that roaring stream, whipping it with fly after fly, while R., the foreordained fisherman, was sitting comfortably in a sawmill, and derricking that pair of three-quarter-pounders in through the window! I had ventured more warily than he, and used, if not the same skill, at least the best skill at my command. My conscience was clear, but so was his; and he had had the drier skin and the greater magnanimity and the biggest fish besides. There is much to be said, in a world like ours, for taking the world as you find it and for fishing with a worm.

II

One's memories of such fishing, however agreeable they may be, are not to be identified with a defense of the practice. Yet, after all, the most effective defense of worm-fishing is the concrete recollection of some brook that could be fished best or only in that way, or the image of a particular trout that yielded to the temptation of an angle-worm after you had flicked fly after fly over him in vain. Indeed, half the zest of brook fishing is in your campaign for "individuals," — as the Salvation Army workers say, — not merely for a basketful of fish *qua* fish, but for a series of individual trout which your instinct tells you ought to lurk under that log or be hovering in that ripple. How to get him, by some sportsmanlike process, is the question. If he will rise to some fly in your book, few fishermen will deny that the fly is the more pleasurable weapon. Dainty, luring, beautiful toy, light as thistledown, falling where you will it to fall, holding when the leader tightens and sings like the string of a violin, the artificial fly represents the poetry of angling. Given the gleam of early morning on some wide water, a heavy trout breaking the surface as he curves and plunges, with the fly holding well, with the right sort of rod in your fingers, and the right man in the other end of the canoe, and you perceive how easy is that Emersonian trick of making the pomp of emperors ridiculous.

But angling's honest prose, as represented by the lowly worm, has also its exalted moments. "The last fish I caught was with a worm," says the honest Walton, and so say I. It was the last evening of last August. The dusk was settling deep upon a tiny meadow, scarcely ten rods from end to end.

The rank bog grass, already drenched with dew, bent over the narrow, deep little brook so closely that it could not be fished except with a double-shotted, baited hook, dropped delicately between the heads of the long grasses. Underneath this canopy the trout were feeding, taking the hook with a straight downward tug, as they made for the hidden bank. It was already twilight when I began, and before I reached the black belt of woods that separated the meadow from the lake, the swift darkness of the North Country made it impossible to see the hook. A short half hour's fishing only, and behold nearly twenty good trout derricked into a basket until then sadly empty. Your rigorous fly-fisherman would have passed that grass-hidden brook in disdain, but it proved a treasure for the humble.

Here, indeed, there was no question of individually minded fish, but simply a neglected brook, full of trout which could be reached with the baited hook only. In more open brook fishing it is always a fascinating problem to decide how to fish a favorite pool or ripple, for much depends upon the hour of the day, the light, the height of water, the precise period of the spring or summer. But after one has decided upon the best theoretical procedure, how often the stupid trout prefers some other plan! And when you have missed a fish that you counted upon landing, what solid satisfaction is still possible for you if you are philosopher enough to sit down then and there, eat your lunch, smoke a meditative pipe, and devise a new campaign against that particular fish! To get another rise from him after lunch is a triumph of diplomacy; to land him is nothing short of statesmanship. For sometimes he will jump furiously at a fly, for very devilishness, without ever meaning to take it, and then, wearying suddenly of his gymnastics, he will snatch sulkily at a grasshopper, beetle, or worm. Trout feed upon an extraordinary variety of crawling things, as all fishermen know who practise the useful habit of opening the first two or three fish they catch, to see what food is that day the favorite.

But here, as elsewhere in this world, the best things lie nearest, and there is no bait so killing, week in and week out, as your plain garden or golf-green angleworm.

Walton's list of possible worms is impressive, and his directions for placing them upon the hook have the placid completeness that belonged to his character. Yet in such matters a little nonconformity may be encouraged. No two men or boys dig bait in quite the same way, though all share, no doubt, the singular elation which gilds that grimy occupation with the spirit of romance. The mind is really occupied, not with the wriggling red creatures in the lumps of earth, but with the stout fish which each worm may capture, just as a saint might rejoice in the squalor of this world as a preparation for the glories of the world to come. Nor do any two experienced fishermen hold quite the same theory as to the best mode of baiting the hook. There are a hundred ways, each of them good. As to the best hook for worm-fishing, you will find dicta in every catalogue of fishing tackle, but size and shape and tempering are qualities that should vary with the brook, the season, and the fisherman. Should one use a three-foot leader, or none at all? Whose rods are best for bait-fishing, granted that all of them should be stiff enough in the tip to lift a good fish by dead strain from a tangle of brush or logs?

Such questions, like those pertaining to the boots or coat which one should wear, the style of bait box one should carry, or the brand of tobacco best suited for smoking in the wind, are topics for unending discussion among the serious minded around the camp fire. Much edification is in them, and yet they are but prudential maxims after all. They are mere moralities of the Franklin or Chesterfield variety, counsels of worldly wisdom, but they leave the soul untouched. A man may have them at his fingers' ends and be no better fisherman at bottom; or he may, like R., ignore most of the admitted rules and come home with a full basket. It is a sufficient defense of fishing with a worm to pronounce the truism that no man is a *complete* angler until he has mastered all the modes of angling. Lovely streams, lonely and enticing, but impossible to fish with a fly, await the fisherman who is not too proud to use, with a man's skill, the same unpretentious tackle which he began with as a boy.

III

But ah, to fish with a worm, and then not catch your fish! To fail with a fly is no disgrace: your art may have been impeccable, your patience faultless to the end. But the philosophy of worm-fishing is that of Results, of having something tangible in your basket when the day's work is done. It is a plea for Compromise, for cutting the coat according to the cloth, for taking the world as it actually is. The fly-fisherman is a natural Foe of Compromise. He throws to the trout a certain kind of lure; an they will take it, so; if not, adieu. He knows no middle path.

> This high man, aiming at a million,
> Misses an unit.

The raptures and the tragedies of consistency are his. He is a scorner of the ground. All honor to him! When he comes back at nightfall and says happily, "I have never cast a line more perfectly than I have to-day," it is almost indecent to peek into his creel. It is like rating Colonel Newcome by his bank account.

But the worm-fisherman is no such proud and isolated soul. He is a "low man" rather than a high one; he honestly cares what his friends will think when they look into his basket to see what he has to show for his day's sport. He watches the Foe of Compromise men go stumbling forward and superbly falling, while he, with less inflexible courage, manages to keep his feet. He wants to score, and not merely to give a pretty exhibition of base-running. At the Harvard-Yale football game of 1903 the Harvard team showed superior strength in rushing the ball; they carried it almost to the Yale goal line repeatedly, but they could not, for some reason, take it over. In the instant of absolute need, the Yale line held, and when the Yale team had to score in order to win, they scored. As the crowd streamed out of the Stadium, a veteran Harvard alumnus said: "This news will cause great sorrow in one home I know of, until they learn by to-morrow's papers that the Harvard team *acquitted itself creditably*." Exactly. Given one team bent upon acquitting itself creditably, and another team determined to win, which will be victorious? The stay-at-homes on the Yale campus that day were not curious to know whether their team was acquitting itself creditably, but whether it was winning the game. Every other question than that was to those young Philistines merely a finespun irrelevance. They took the Cash and let the Credit go.

There is much to be said, no doubt, for the Harvard veteran's point of view. The proper kind of credit may be a better asset for eleven boys than any championship; and to fish a bit of water consistently and skillfully, with your best flies and in your best manner, is perhaps achievement enough. So says the Foe of Compromise, at least. But the Yale spirit will be prying into the basket in search of fish; it prefers concrete results. If all men are by nature either Platonists or Aristotelians, fly-fishermen or worm-fishermen, how difficult it is for us to do one another justice! Differing in mind, in aim and method, how shall we say infallibly that this man or that is wrong? To fail with Plato for companion may be better than to succeed with Aristotle. But one thing is perfectly clear: there is no warrant for Compromise but in success. Use a worm if you will, but you must have fish to show for it, if you would escape the finger of scorn. If you find yourself camping by an unknown brook and are deputed to catch the necessary trout for breakfast, it is wiser to choose the surest bait. The crackle of the fish in the frying pan will atone for any theoretical defect in your method. But to choose the surest bait, and then to bring back no fish, is unforgivable. Forsake Plato if you must — but you may do so only at the price of justifying yourself in the terms of Aristotelian arithmetic. The college president who abandoned his college in order to run a cotton mill was free to make his own choice of a calling; but he was never pardoned for bankrupting the mill. If one is bound to be a low man rather than an impractical idealist, he should at least make sure of his vulgar success.

Is all this but a disguised defense of pot-hunting? No. There is no possible defense of pot-hunting, whether it be upon a trout brook or in the stock market. Against fish or men, one should play the game fairly. Yet for that matter some of the most skillful fly-fishermen I have known were pot-hunters at heart, and some of the most prosaic-looking merchants were idealists compared to whom Shelley was but a dreaming boy. All depends upon the spirit with which one makes his venture. I recall a boy of five who gravely watched his father tramp off after rabbits — gun on shoulder and beagle in leash. Thereupon he shouldered a wooden sword and, dragging his reluctant black kitten by a string, sallied

forth upon the dusty Vermont road "to
get a lion for breakfast." That is the true
sporting temper! Let there be but a fine
idealism in the quest, and the particular
object is unessential. "A true fisherman's
happiness," says Mr. Cleveland, "is not
dependent upon his luck." It depends upon
his heart.

No doubt all amateur fishing is but
"play," as the psychologists soberly term
it: not a necessary, but a freely assumed
activity, born of surplusage of vitality.
Nobody, not even a carpenter wearied of
his job, has to go fishing unless he wants to.
He may indeed find himself breakfastless in
camp, and obliged to betake himself to the
brook — but then he need not have gone
into the woods at all. Yet if he does decide
to fish, let him

> Venture as warily, use the same skill,
> Do his best —

whatever variety of tackle he may choose.
He can be a whole-souled sportsman with
the poorest equipment, or a mean "trout
hog" with the most elaborate.

Only, in the name of gentle Izaak himself, let him be a *complete* angler; and let the man be a passionate amateur of all the arts of life, despising none of them, and using all of them for his soul's good and for the joy of his fellows. If he be, so to speak, but a worm-fisherman, — a follower of humble occupations, and pledged to unromantic duties, — let him still thrill with the pleasures of the true sportsman. To make the most of dull hours, to make the best of dull people, to like a poor jest better than none, to wear the threadbare coat like a gentleman, to be outvoted with a smile, to hitch your wagon to the old horse if no star is handy — this is the wholesome philosophy taught by fishing with a worm. The fun of it depends upon the heart. There may be as much zest in saving as in spending, in working for small wages as for great, in avoiding the snapshots of publicity as in being invariably first "among those present." But a man should be honest. If he catches most of his fish with a worm, secures the larger portion of his success by commonplace industry, let him glory in it, for this, too, is part of the great game. Yet he ought not in that case to pose as a fly-fisherman only — to carry himself as one aware of the immortalizing camera, to pretend that life is easy if one but knows how to drop a fly into the right ripple. For life is not easy, after all is said. It is a long brook to fish, and it needs a stout heart and a wise patience. All the flies there are in the book, and all the bait that can be carried in the box, are likely to be needed ere the day is over. But, like the Psalmist's "river of God," this brook is "full of water," and there is plenty of good fishing to be had in it if one is neither afraid nor ashamed of fishing sometimes with a worm.

FISHING WITH A FLY

FISHING WITH A FLY

I

I CONFESS that I am a fisherman of little or no reputation. Whatever good repute I might conceivably have won I forfeited, more than a score of years ago, by writing — and accepting — for the *Atlantic* an essay on "Fishing with a Worm." I shall never live down that essay. No matter what fish I have brought proudly home since then, — brook trout or rainbows, brown trout or gray, sea trout or salmon, — there is always some cynical friend to insinuate that I probably caught them with a worm! I shall never rehabilitate myself, not even if the present editor of the *Atlantic* takes pity on me and prints these meditations upon the art and mystery of fishing with a fly.

That old essay had at least the merit of honesty — a virtue not always attributed to fishermen. It admitted that fly-fishing is the finer art, wherever fly-fishing is to be had. It claimed merely that on waters where such fishing is impracticable there is much to be said for making the best of the situation and using the despised and wriggling worm. I hope that this paper will be equally honest, and I shall therefore unburden myself with a second confession, namely, that I am only a mediocre practitioner of the art which I am now attempting to praise. This is no Halford or Hewitt! The critic in me reports of the angler in me: —

"I have watched that fellow fishing, on and off, for fifty years. He has never learned to make his own flies. He ties a clumsy knot. He uses too heavy leaders. He sticks to that old warped Leonard rod because it once belonged to Dr. James O. Murray, though he has far better ones in his rod case. He gets fair distance in casting, especially with a two-handed salmon-rod, but his wrist is not quite supple enough. I consider him poor with the dry fly. He seems really happier when fishing with a wet fly downstream, like the Early Victorians. But I have actually seen him kill good trout, fishing across-stream, with a dry fly on the dropper and a wet one for the tail fly: a method entirely illogical. He is superstitious about his choice of flies. He pays too much attention to his hunches and too little to the natural flies to which the trout happen to be rising. I call him obstinate. He plays a small fish well enough, but he gets flurried with the big ones. He nets other men's fish much better than his own. He takes foolish chances in shooting rapids and climbing slippery rocks and wading salmon rivers in flood. I wouldn't grade him A or even B. About a C+."

Critics are always right, even when they miss the point. The point is that the fun and glory of fishing consist in fishing, and not in being "high rod." The men with whom I have had the happiest days on various rivers — L. the painter and A. the oculist, and C. E. B. C. the D.D.S. — are far more delicate fly-fishermen than I shall ever be. For that matter, L. B., a village blacksmith in Cape Breton, whom I left sorrowfully shoeing a horse one Saturday afternoon last July when he had promised to fish the Forks pool with me, has a more delicate hand than any of them when it comes to fishing "far and fine." But the whole spirit of competition is alien to the true angler's mood. What difference does it make whose basket is heaviest? Everyone likes his share of luck, of course, — his to-day and another man's to-morrow, — but when you go fishing you are dealing with what Royce used to call the Absolute. All relativities are irrelevant.

It is for this reason that even the clumsiest angler may record his guesses at the secret of the peculiar satisfaction which fly-fishing affords. Guesses they must remain, for no one can give an adequate explanation. "Exactly what is the nature of this pleasure which you find in smoking?" President Eliot once asked me with benignant skepticism. I did not pass that examination very well. I doubt if any smoker can. But your fly-fisherman, at least, is voluble enough in his own defense. (Give him a moment first, to light his pipe!)

For one thing, — and this is a consid-

eration which might appeal to President
Eliot, a veteran champion of training of
the eye and hand, — fly-fishing calls for the
most precise and fastidious manipulation
of exquisitely fashioned tools. A three- or
four-ounce split-bamboo rod, with a well-
balanced reel, a tapered casting-line, a
leader of the proper fineness, and a well-tied
fly or flies, is one of the most perfectly
designed and executed triumphs of human
artisanship. A violin is but little better.
At its pitch of dainty perfection it delights
both the eye and the tactile sense, for not
every rod which is beautifully made has the
crowning virtue of the right "feel." And
that it should look right and feel right as it
comes to you from the skilled workman is
only a part of the visual and manual pleasure which it yields. For you, with your
quite individual bodily and mental habits,
your slowly acquired art as a fisherman,
must now use this fragile combination of
wood and steel and silk and gut and feathers
under the most subtly variable conditions of
light, wind, and water. You must be able

to cast with either hand, in every imaginable posture, and under all mental conditions of exaltation or fatigue. Most trout that are hooked are struck within twenty-five or thirty feet of the fisherman, but on occasion you will wish to cast twice that distance or even more. And there is no moment of a long day on brook, river, or lake, whether your creel is filling or empty, when you are not conscious of the rich pleasure of using an instrument which is beautiful and exquisite in itself.

The very artificiality of the means employed heightens the enjoyment of fly-fishing. You choose deliberately the lightest tackle that will hold the fish. Perhaps you use a barbless hook, to increase the odds against you. At any rate, you give the fish a sporting chance. You neither net nor spear nor dynamite him. You challenge him to a trial of wits, his against yours. It does not become me to speak disrespectfully of the man who drops a fat worm, anchored to a steel rod, under the nose of some trout lurking in a bushy tangle of the brook, and "derricks" him on to the bank. I have done it too often! And there are exciting minutes in striking a big "laker" seventy feet below the surface, or in trolling with a minnow or spinner for pike or landlocked salmon. Nevertheless, if a fish has been well hooked under such conditions, with powerful tackle, it is all up with him. He has little or no chance. But when a rainbow or brook or sea trout — and above all a fresh-run salmon — takes the fly the struggle is only begun. The lighter the tackle the greater the margin of uncertainty, and of glory if you win. Every angler who has had a sea trout weighing a pound or two rise accidentally to his salmon fly when he was fishing with a fifteen-foot, two-handed rod knows the disappointing, unsportsmanlike sensation of reeling in the unlucky fish. Yet that very same sea trout on a three-ounce rod would have given noble and uncertain battle. Mr. Cleveland used to argue with me that a black bass, pound for pound, was a better fighter than a trout. He was a sturdier debater than I, and a far more experienced bass-fisherman; but if I can have a four-pound grilse on a four-ounce rod in fast water, anybody may have the bass.

Surely nothing can be more artificial, and few things more beautiful, than a man-made fly. I shall not enter upon the interminable question of the relative advantages of the fly made in exact imitation of the natural insect, versus the fly which imitates, like the Jock Scott or the Durham Ranger, no creature that ever existed. Trout and salmon rise to both of these kinds of flies — and sometimes to neither! The best debate I ever heard on this fascinating subject took place one July night in an inn on Baker's River, between a Concord parson who fished with nothing but a wet fly tied most cunningly by himself, and a Boston architect who fished with nothing but a dry fly — that is, a precise copy of a real fly, made to float upright within the field of vision of a special trout who on that day or hour is feeding upon the real fly in question. The umpire of the debate was an itinerant piano-tuner, whom I suspected of being a worm-fisherman at heart. When we finally agreed to smoke a last pipe and turn in — the only thing on which we could agree at all — I ventured to ask the parson how his wet flies had worked that day. It had been bright and hot, with low water.

"I did n't get anything," confessed the parson.

"How about you?" I asked the architect.

"Nor I either," replied the dry-fly expert.

Now I had been fishing, first with a wet fly, and then with a dry fly, and my luck was exactly the same as theirs!

"Well," said the piano-tuner, by way of closing the discussion, "can any of you fellows sing? I kind o' like a little music before I go to bed. Do you know that hotel at Woodsville?"

I remarked that it was the one celebrated by Robert Frost in the poem entitled "A Hundred Collars."

"Very likely," assented the piano-tuner, vaguely. "Well, I was sitting there one night and there was a troupe of singers that had come down from Montreal, waiting for the Boston sleeper. One of those fellows was trying to transpose something on the piano. I says, 'Here, I'll transpose that for you, and you see if you can sing it.' So I sat down to the piano and he began to sing. Say, now, *my gorry!* He *could* sing! I've got his card yet. He spelled his name B-i-s-p-h-a-m. And before he got through a woman came down from upstairs and said she guessed *she* would sing too. Say! By midnight we had two hundred people trying to crowd into that hotel to hear her! Her name was Eames."

And so, each with his own memories of those golden vanished voices, we fishermen crept quietly upstairs to bed — and the debate was never settled.

II

But surely a clear majority of anglers are ready to admit that fly-fishing, in addition to the singular charm which arises from the nature of its artistry, affords also an unrivaled satisfaction in its opportunities for studying the habits and behavior of noble species of fish. For there is an embryo scientist, as well as an humble artist, in every outdoors man. The fly-fisherman, through long practice in alert observation, develops not only the sea gull's or fish hawk's vision for what is below the surface of the water, but also a kind of sixth sense for what the fish themselves are seeing and thinking. He learns that what really matters is not the color and shape of the fly as the fisherman looks down at it in his fly book or upon the surface of the stream, but the color and shape and reflection of light as these appear to the eyes of a fish looking at the fly from underneath in moving water. Many recent books on the dry fly have printed curiously interesting photographs, made underneath specially constructed glass-bottomed fish-tanks, with the camera pointed upward, so that every motion of the rising trout, as the fly floats within his sharply limited angle of vision, is easily registered. It is demonstrable that familiar patterns of flies, photographed from below through several feet of running water, and thus giving the object as it appears to the fish rather than to the fisherman, present this whole subject of trout psychology in a new light.

The problem, obviously, is to offer to the trout something pleasing to him, and not at all something which happens to tickle your own human fancy in patterns and colors. It is as if a necktie which suits you may not appeal to your wife's taste in the least! A year ago I fished a tiny lake in northern Quebec. "You'll find," said a friendly lumberman, "that they'll take just one fly: a Parmachenee Belle, No. 6"; and as I had nothing of that size in that pattern, he gave me a couple. I tried half a dozen other flies first, and had a few rises to a Dark Montreal, but the real fishing did not begin until I put on those big gaudy red-and-white No. 6's. Now precisely why should those trout, very rarely fished over, demand that special stimulus to sense perception?

Take another instance. Last July A. and I were fishing a stream in Nova Scotia, where I had never failed to take plenty of small trout. We were planning, in fact, to lunch on trout, with some incidental coffee and bacon and toast. It was long after noon when we reached the chosen spot, and I was sure that a quarter of an hour's fishing would provide the luncheon. To my dismay we could not take a single trout. A whole baffling hungry hour went by. Then A., who had been changing flies every few minutes, put on a tiny brown hackle. In ten minutes he took more trout than we could eat. Now why?

Or why, after lunch that day, did the trout change their minds again? It was three o'clock, sunny, windless, and very hot, when I reached a strip of dead water, about three feet deep, thirty yards wide, and perhaps a hundred yards long, lined with thick alders. Near the foot of this dead water, as I peered through the alders, I saw, in full glaring sunlight, not a dozen feet away, a school of good-sized trout. Instinctively I dropped to my knees in the wet sedge grass. I had just broken the tip of a new and very light rod, in striking a three-quarter pounder, and though he was flapping in the basket the hastily spliced tip would not bear the slightest strain. The alders were so close behind me that a decent backcast was impossible. In fact everything was wrong, except that I had not yet frightened the trout. I put on a No. 12 Silver Doctor and, prayerfully favoring the broken tip, managed to flick a nondescript backhanded, underhand cast so as to reach the fish, who were still not fifteen feet upstream. *Thump!* The tip held, and the net was under him; and so it went — *thump! thump!* — for a quarter of an hour, my aching knees sinking lower and lower into the mud, and the little Silver Doctor working magically, until ten of the prize scholars in that school had been promoted to the basket: more fish and bigger fish than I have often taken in a whole day's sport under the most favorable conditions. And it is only fair to add that A., fifty yards upstream, balanced on a little flat rock just below a cold brook that ran into the dead water, and fishing with a tiny brown dry fly which neither of us could identify, took even more trout that afternoon than I did — most of them actually in his own shadow, as the dry fly floated downstream toward him.

No, there is simply no understanding the mysteries of a trout's eye and mind. Their habits seem so fixed that learned scientists can write books about them; and then all at once they go plunging off their orbit in some subaqueous brainstorm. The best fly-fishing I ever expect to have was during a September snow squall, well up toward Hudson's Bay. The rise lasted about half an hour, and W. and I, shivering in the bottom of the rocking canoes, in a gale of wind, took seventeen brook trout, mostly males in superb color and condition, weighing altogether just under twenty pounds. Was it hunger, or the excitement of the snowstorm agitating the shallow water, or some occult mob psychology that defies analysis, that made them rise so feverishly?

Equally fascinating is the behavior of individual fish under more normal circumstances. Are trout more shy, or less shy, in water that is constantly fished? Anglers differ widely in answering this apparently simple question. The upper ten miles of the Lamoille, for instance, are fished certainly once a day by someone during the whole season. I have fished that delightful river for twenty-five years, though never with much luck. The trout are getting scarcer each year, — thanks to the motor cars, — but I cannot see that the fish are more shy or less shy than they are in some inaccessible streams that are fished only once or twice a summer. But there are always individual trout who contradict every usual law of their habitat. These mavericks who will not run with the herd, who are cautious when others are bold and bold when others are cautious, who are full of whims and humors, incite the fly-fisherman to his most cunning devices. They are hard to raise, hard to hook, and hard to bring to the net. If you can capture a couple of these experienced old cynics in an afternoon, you have a right to be proud.

I met on the Margaree last summer a Scotchman from Inverness who holds that no two salmon are alike in their feelings or behavior. In his selection of flies, it is true, he has gone to the extreme of simplification. He fishes with nothing but a Black Dose in the morning hours, and a Jock Scott or Silver Doctor toward evening, and, like a true Scot, he prefers a single-pointed hook. During the season of 1923, he hooked nineteen salmon in the overfished open water of the Margaree, and brought seventeen of them to the gaff — a very high average of performance, for ordinarily, if you land one salmon to every two that you hook and three that you raise, you are doing well enough. He claimed that no two of his seventeen salmon behaved in anything like the same fashion. He had to alter his strategy and tactics for each individual case, obeying the infinite variety of conditioning circumstances in each pool, as well as the varying moods, resources, and fighting-quality of each fish. But I have fished that same river with an Italian wine merchant, a notoriously lucky angler, whose sole theory seems to be, after hooking a salmon, to "treat him rough"; that is, to give him the full pressure of a heavy rod, and reel him in without ceremony. The Scotchman seems to me, however, a finer metaphysician than the countryman of Saint Francis, Savonarola, and Mussolini, and a happier fisherman, though he may not kill any more fish.

III

An American treatise on æsthetics, in distinguishing between higher and lower pleasures, makes much of the point that the higher æsthetic impressions are permanently pleasurable in revival. Many fly-fishermen will agree with me in thinking that some of their most unalloyed happiness is in their memory of the circumstances attending the capture — or even the loss! — of some one fish. No one ever forgot his first trout! I can see myself yet, backing off a couple of rods from the brook in the Heart of Greylock, — it was then in spring flood, — squeezing in two boyish fists that black and slippery miracle, and not daring to take him off the hook for fear he might escape!

But that first trout, like Izaak Walton's last one, was caught with a worm. In June of that year, however, I saw for the first time a trout taken on a fly. A schoolmate, with such a dainty rod as I had never dreamed of, was fishing a deep, willow-shadowed pool just below the junction of the Ashford and Hancock brooks in South Williamstown. It was after sunset, and he was casting deftly under the willows with a white fly, when suddenly a trout leaped for it, and after a few desperate plunges was drawn coolly up on the gravel bank. It weighed exactly a pound. The captor affected to make little of his triumph; but I noticed that he presented the trout, with his compliments, to "Miss Blanche."

Forty-nine years ago, and the boy's name and face are long since forgotten, but the June dusk and the dark rippling water and the white fly and the gleaming rush of that big trout excite me still! What moments one recalls! That dawn on the Miramichi, and the gorgeously colored two-pound trout that raced a grilse for my tiny double-pointed Jock Scott, and beat the grilse by an inch! That other two-pounder at the foot of one of the Marteau lakes, at midday in full September sunshine, curving up grandly to a Montreal on a very long cast and fighting up and down the fifty-foot pool like a salmon! The leaping rainbow in the granite basin on Baker's River! The grilse hooked by Donald as we were standing on the top of the old dam on the Clearwater, when Donald — showing off a little, as guides sometimes will — cast eighty feet downstream into a little amber-colored pool where the grilse took the fly, and I played him from the top of the dam while Donald climbed down and gaffed him! So clear were that marvelous air and still more marvelous water that I could almost count the spots upon the grilse's flashing sides.

And here comes one of the paradoxes of fishing. By some strange trick of the memory, the fish which you take or lose seem in retrospect only a bit of high light in the general picture. The exaltation of an instant of perfect skill, the heartbreaking sense of clumsiness or stupidity when you lose a salmon, lessen their poignancy in the presence of the beauty which is always waiting upon the angler. The cardinal flowers blooming twenty years ago on a mossy log upon the shadowed shore of Big Greenough Pond are lovely yet, though not a trout rose that morning from under the log. The big red fox still squats on his haunches upon the far side of Norbert's Pool, wisely criticizing my unsuccessful casting. The ravens bark hoarsely in the black spruces above the Sheerdam. That pair of great horned owls still follow me down the Olmsted brook. The buck that snorted and jumped just behind me as I was making a very careful cast on the Big Magalloway still makes my heart pump — so silent was that lonely afternoon. The moose tracks are still there on the muddy shore of the St. Maurice. The cries of strange birds in the twilight haunt the willow copses along the Margaree. The endless hot afternoons on the Miramichi, while we were waiting for falling water, are no longer tedious, for now they are crowded with pictures of friendly purple finches, and mother partridges with their broods, and "mourning-cloak" butterflies clustering by thousands upon the worn rocks by the river. No, you may forget the fish that you catch or lose, but you can never forget the fishing!

I have no quarrel with the persons who go into the woods to peep and botanize and name all the birds without a gun. There is fun enough in this world, if properly distributed, to give everybody something. But I am stating a truism when I claim that the man with a rod or gun sees more and feels more in the woods than if he were to go empty-handed. In moments of tense excitement in watching for fish or game one's field of vision is wider and sight and hearing are more sensitive than in any moods of mere passive receptivity to "Nature's teaching." Never is the dawn more miraculous than when the fog first lifts along the reaches of the river and you tie on a favorite fly with chilled, fumbling fingers, light your first pipe of the day, and wade, shivering,

into the chuckling water. Never is the divine
and terrifying mystery of the dark so close
to you as when you are stumbling campward
in the twilight along an unknown trail. The
woodsman who cannot understand how a
man can be panic-stricken by the dark is no
woodsman. He lacks a sense of the situation: of the very narrow line that separates
fire, food, and shelter from the desperate
horror of "a man lost." I helped find one of
these men once. He rose up gaunt in the
October dusk from a bog back of Spencer
Mountain, and waved his arms wildly just
as I was holding the rifle on him, taking him
for a moose; and I shall never forget how we
filled him up with coffee, trout, and venison
that night, and put him safely on the "tote
road" in the morning.

And between dawn and dark what infinite variations of air and light and color
and wind play upon the mind of the fisherman as if it were an opal ! The wind caresses
him one moment, and torments him the
next, tossing his fly into treetops or breaking
the brittle hook against a rock. But the

water is the true opal. In the upper reaches of many of our New England streams the water flowing from a peat bog or cedar swamp has the tone of a very dark sherry; in full sunlight, flecked by shadows, it becomes one of Emerson's leopard-colored rills; as it pours over granite ledges it changes to something strangely austere and pure. No two successive hours are alike to the angler, for the brook or river is changing its form and hue in every instant, and his mind and mood and artistry are affected by every yard of the gliding, Protean stream. He is watching it, not with the sentimentalist's preoccupation with pure beauty, but rather with the fisherman's trained perception of the effect of wind and light, of deeper or darker-colored water, of eddy or shallow, upon the next cast of his fly. The paradox is that this very preoccupation with angling seems to make him more sensitive to the enfolding beauty of the landscape.

He must, of course, to perceive it fully, have a certain capacity for philosophical detachment, a kind of Oriental superiority to failure or success. Perhaps that is what being a "born fisherman" means. A. and I, a few months ago, started out to fish a famous salmon-pool. Three or four salmon could be seen lying there, dark wavering shapes in ten or fifteen feet of water. On the gravel bank above them, precisely where we had expected to take turns casting, stood an elderly gentleman who had already been fishing for three hours on that same spot. I hope it was not mere envy of his prior occupation of the coveted "stand" which made us rate him as the worst fisherman in the world. He slapped the water petulantly with a line that reached not halfway to the sulking fish; he jerked the fly out before it had a chance to float down with the current, and nervously slapped it back again. We watched him for a whole hour, and then went around him down the river. It was an enchanting afternoon, in the loveliest of valleys. We fished our prettiest, using every device known to us, but raised nothing, and by sunset we had worked back to the pool and learned what had happened.

After nearly seven hours of persistent thrashing and jerking and thrashing on that one spot, a salmon — either irritated at last beyond endurance or driven by some obscure suicidal mania — had actually risen to that duffer's fly, and been hooked, played, and gaffed! Weight, twenty-two pounds.

I must have looked what I felt. "Never mind," said A. "Let him have his fish. You and I have had a richer day than he." Was it a born fisherman's infinite capacity for self-deception, or was it a real insight into the nature of happiness, that made us tramp upstream again, proud as two Spanish grandees, without tangible possessions, but rich in memory and in hope? As for the elderly gentleman, he did not need any philosophy. He had his salmon.

But this sense of personal prowess in killing fish or game is certainly a curious trait in civilized elderly gentlemen. Is it, as some persons believe, a survival of savagery, a reversion to primitivism? Is the distinction between killing fish and killing game a real one? Many men make it. They can no longer shoot a gray squirrel or a rabbit or partridge or even a deer; they now prefer to watch them. But they will still catch fish and shoot ducks; "ducks being different," as C. E. B. C. says. Note that they do not really need either fish or ducks for food. In fact, any fisherman who has been caught in the woods with supplies running low and has been obliged to kill fish or go hungry will tell you that angling under such circumstances loses most of its fascination. There is too much primitivism in it, and not enough illusion. But mark how narrow is the margin of pleasurable sport! If you need the fish for food, your pure pleasure in taking them diminishes. And on the other hand, when there is no question at all of actual necessity and you have simply felt like going fishing, you become conscious at some late hour upon a lucky day that you have taken "your share" of fish. After that moment your pleasure swiftly evaporates; you feel unsportsmanlike in killing any more. Is not the mentality of fishermen unaccountable?

IV

There is one aspect of this reversion to primitivism, however, which is very real, and of inestimable value to sedentary gentlemen. A fishing trip somehow taps in them unsuspected reservoirs of physical and moral energy. They may habitually put on rubbers when they walk to the post office in damp weather; they consult throat specialists; they seriously consider being examined by a life-extension institute. And here they are suddenly swinging off the Winnipeg Pullman at midnight at a flag station, with duffle bag, rod case, and rifle, to be greeted taciturnly by guides whom they have never seen but who will know them in a week better than they know themselves. They will forget all about their rubbers and their throats and the admonitions of their wives. They will wade waist-deep in icy water and crouch for hours under dripping hemlocks. At home they expect a "red-cap" to carry their suitcase and a chauffeur to open the door of their car; but here they cheerfully tote a bushel of potatoes over a hard portage if the guide has all he can do with the canoe. They can eat anything, drink anything, smoke anything, — except the native Canadian tobacco! — and crawl at night into a dirty sleeping bag as if it were the couch of an emperor. A life-extension institute? Did not Izaak Walton live to be ninety, and did not Henry M.'s uncle, when the ice went out of the Miramichi below Boisetown in the spring of 1922, celebrate his hundredth birthday by casting the whole day for black salmon? Nonsense! If the rod and reel are working well, and the fly book is wisely filled, and the sky a bit overcast, and there is just enough ripple on the water, your life-extension institute is already functioning!

The mystery of fly-fishing, after all, is what is called by the younger generation a "complex." One of its strands — not the subtlest — is mere joy in manual dexterity. Another is the exquisite artificiality with which the means are adapted to the end. There is the pleasure of accurate observation of bewildering living creatures. There is moving water, and all the changes of the sky, shadow and sunlight and raindrops upon trees and flowers, and the old, inexhaustible, indescribable beauty of the world. There are a few fish. There is at times the zest of companionship and at other times the satisfaction of solitude. There are gentle memories of some "excellent angler, now with God." And always there is that deep secret of expectation, the vital energy, ever strangely renewed, which looks for some fulfillment of its dreams beyond the next height of land, below the next turn of the stream. There are no scales for weighing such imponderable things as these, but surely next to the happiness of one's own home and work is the happiness of sitting in the bow of a canoe, rod in hand, as the guide paddles you noiselessly around the bend of an unknown river. Life offers few moments more thrilling than that, and one may be permitted to think that Death will not offer anything very different.

REVISITING A RIVER

REVISITING A RIVER

To revisit a river is like trying to redream a dream. You are aware, of course, that you have changed and that the river must have changed and that no two dreams are precisely alike. Yet the identities are more profound than the differences, and the moment you are on the stream you have the old illusion of timelessness. This mortal has put on immortality. Some hundreds of miles to the south of you your secretary is saying firmly: "No, he cannot be reached by telephone or letters or telegrams. He expects to come out in about a month." There may be other ways of securing such absolute freedom from this most relative of worlds, but if a man has sense enough to know when he is happy, is there anything like that moment when the guide has packed the duffle bags and rods and tent and provisions into the canoe, seen that she trims well with your weight in the bow, and pushes off! *"Au large!"* he may exclaim if he is a Frenchman. If he is an

Indian or a dour Scot he will e'en just say
nothing. But what is there to say? The
cup is full.

I

Let us have a little geography, but not
too much. The river which I am revisiting
after five years' absence is in New Brunswick, and where we take the water we are
one hundred and fifty miles from the sea
and fifty miles above "the settlements,"
with only two rough hunting and fishing
shacks on that stretch of fifty miles. The
river is the only road. There are larger
streams in the Province, and a few where
the salmon and sea trout are heavier, but
none that runs through wilder country.
On the Crown Lands map you will find
the region of C. E. B. C.'s camp indicated
by the words "Tungsten and Salmon" in
red letters. But the tungsten mine, worked
for a time during the World War, is now
abandoned, and a saturnine hedgehog, the
sole watchman over all that costly machin-
ery, lies curled on the rotting rafters above

the main shaft. Prospectors for gold and radium have come here likewise, but they are all gone now, like the caribou. Once or twice a week, during the summer months, a fisherman's canoe slips up or down the river, and in October there are a few hunters in quest of moose and bear.

Two of the three guides waiting for us are old friends. All three are Scotchmen, born and bred on this river, like their fathers and grandfathers before them, lumbering in the winter, driving logs in the spring, guiding fishermen in the short summers, and hunting in the fall. They are a wiry, tough breed, used to what they call "brutin' work," though there is not much of that in store for them at Burnt Hill, whither we are bound.

I miss the log canoes this year — those old thirty-foot dugouts, hollowed from a single stick of pine. Down by the settlements you still see a few of them, but almost never a new one. The primeval pines were burned in the great fire that swept up the river a century ago, and, though the pines are slowly coming back, there are few big enough to make a dugout. But these log canoes were steady, strong, and good for thirty or forty years of rough work. Poled by two men, they are surprisingly quick in the water; indeed, this very summer we were visited by a tall, lean guide who had poled his "log" alone twenty-nine miles up river in five hours and a half. Fast going! And you can stand up in them to cast for salmon far more securely than in a canvas canoe.

Our three canvases, this year, are shod on the outside with extra longitudinal ribs to protect them in this rockiest of rivers. The water is low, and the bigger rapids, though seemingly less formidable than usual, require dexterous poling as well as that special knowledge of channels and currents which is the priceless inheritance of guides who have spent their whole lives upon one stream. You do not realize their expertness until you watch canoes manned by good men, though strange to this river, pick their way cautiously through the fast water by our camp. They may be Frenchmen or Indians or Tobique or St. John men, seasoned guides, of course, who can be trusted even in new territory to pick up a trail or find a spring. But how gingerly they pole past Orr's Rock and Dyer's Hole and the Lower Pitch! This is no job for a mere general practitioner. It calls for a specialist.

Were the salmon already running up? Yes! That strange wireless telegraphy by which every dweller on a salmon stream knows precisely who killed the fish this morning — perhaps forty miles away — is working accurately. And there are reports of a big run of grilse, too, a grilse being a three-year-old salmon, making his first trip back from salt water to his native river. Last season he was only a four- or five-inch parr, swarming in every trout brook that pours into a salmon river, and often rising voraciously to a salmon fly in the river itself. But now, after only a few months in the Atlantic, he weighs from three to six pounds, and every ounce of him is full of fight.

As we slip downstream, watching warily for everything from a mink to a moose, it is evident that the season is two or three weeks late. Pale wild roses are still in bloom, and blue iris. Bluebells are waving everywhere in the crevices of the gray rocks, and the pink sheep laurel covers the sunnier, higher ledges. Not a huckleberry yet anywhere. My guide whispers: "On the right; way down!" and there is the first deer, with his head quite under water as he munches the short green moss on the submerged rocks. There is the first fish hawk, and when we go ashore for lunch and pull a trout rod from the case and make the first cast after many a month of abstinence — *bang!* There is the first squaretail! C. E. B. C., whose canoe is ahead of G.'s and mine, is lucky enough, as we near Burnt Hill, to see a huge black bear standing up on his hind legs by the shore — the very bear, perhaps, that sneaked into the camp last year and stole all the fresh doughnuts.

We round the last bend of the river,

catch the steady roar of Burnt Hill Brook
on the left, shoot the last rapids, and
there — as if we had left it only yester-
day — is the old camp, a fishing shack
built thirty years ago for Joseph Jefferson.
"Mr." Jefferson, I notice the older guides
say, and never "Joe." They were very
fond of him, though he had stern preju-
dices against spearing salmon by torch-
light and shooting deer out of season. On
the east end of the porch — where the
boards are gnawed by hedgehogs and split
off by hunters in too great a hurry, on
October evenings, to get a fire started in
the cookstove inside the cabin — thousands
of salmon have been flung down. A few of
the biggest have had their outlines rudely
carved on boards, nailed up outside and
inside the cabin, with the captor's name
and the date. Two women fishermen, in
gracious recognition of the rights of the
owner of these best pools on the river,
have added the words "By courtesy of
C. E. B. C." Laurence Hutton, a friend of
Mr. Jefferson and of nearly everybody else,

used to say that there was one difference between persons even more marked than Charles Lamb's distinction between the men who borrow and the men who lend — the difference, namely, between those who forget to say "Thank you" and those who remember.

The twilights are long here, and after the tents were pitched on the bluff and supper eaten in the cabin there was light enough to hook — and lose — the first salmon. As it slowly darkened, the nighthawks began to circle above the stream, the deer stole out to drink, and the ripples along the faster water began to weave their fantastic patterns of black velvet shot with silver. A whippoorwill, the first I remember hearing as far north as this, is calling from the white birches behind the tents. The thermometer registers 43, and we crawl into our sleeping bags and listen for a few happy minutes to the roar of the river — and the next thing I know a golden-coated three-year-old buck is pawing and snorting just outside the tent, in the broad morning sunshine. We have come home.

II

How wayward are a fisherman's memories! I recall that buck far more vividly than the first day's fishing, and indeed I have to turn to the log book to discover that for three or four days the fishing was hardly worth recording. The water was still falling and the days were bright and hot. I watched for certain friends made on the previous trip, and found the marvelous clusters of mourning-cloak butterflies still circling about the hollows of the ledges, just out of reach of the rapids. There was a great flight of big yellow Turnus butterflies also. The kingfishers still haunt the river, flying, G. says, "as if they were going somewhere." But the purple finches that used to swarm about the cabin five years ago have dwindled to a single pair. The rabbits are not so friendly, and there is not a partridge to be seen.

There are hours in these long tranquil days when salmon fishing is a fierce obsession, and you cast greedily, insatiably; but there are other hours when all you seem to want is to watch the butterflies on the rocks, to try to recall the names of plants, and to bewail your general ignorance. "The advantage of going into the woods," said a Maine guide to me once, "is that you learn something new each day." That is true enough, but what you learn is pitifully small compared with what you would like to learn. The guides can set you straight on rare varieties of trees, for they are born lumbermen, but I have never known one possessed of more than a child's knowledge of birds and flowers. This river is one of the richest fields for a mineralogist, but the guides know only that the quartz veins begin a couple of miles above the camp, and that schist and granite are just schist and granite. An angler ought really to be rich enough to lead a captive botanist and ornithologist and geologist in his train to answer questions — provided they would not complain too much of the black flies, and would keep out of the way of his backcast!

No angler could ask for better company,

it is true, than G. and C. E. B. C. They
sit on the cabin porch for hours during the
glaring middle of the day, discoursing
learnedly about the relative advantages of
Hoff and Hardy reels, and the precise number of ounces that a dry-fly salmon rod
should weigh, and whether a certain im-
ported English line is really too light or
too heavy for a certain Leonard rod. They
know all about knots. They have read the
latest treatises on fishing. Their fly books
are a Paradise of Dainty Devices, and they
argue amiably about patterns and sizes and
double-pointed hooks and all the other tangible aspects of this old art and mystery of
angling. It is with unfeigned humility,
after listening to them, that I reach into
the pocket of a disreputable fishing coat,
faded with the rains and sunshine of a
dozen summers, and pull out a cheap water-
stained fly book which I have carried for
thirty years. Alas, I find that I am short
of this or that approved pattern for the
day, and that I cannot remember the names
of half the flies in the book. Worse yet, I

am secretly aware that there are some
battered lucky flies there, on which I have
killed fish year after year, although I know
well enough that the loops are liable to pull
out if I strike a heavy salmon. I ought, of
course, to weed them out, and have a new
pigskin book, properly filled with this
year's flies, all as neatly arranged as a
museum. And I ought to sort my leaders
more carefully, and record the exact number of pounds each is warranted to pull.
I am getting lower and lower in my mind.
To think that I once ventured to grade
myself as a "C+" fisherman! "D—"
would be nearer the truth.

III

Just then, curiously enough, my guide
Henry passes the porch, axe in hand and
a young birch tree — for firewood — balanced on his shoulder. As I recall something Henry happened to say last night,
my humility alters suddenly into a whim-
sical, inverted pride. I had lent him my
rod, to see if he could hook a fish that I

had raised once but could not tempt again. Henry tacitly hooked and landed him, as simply as if there were no approved theories to be observed and it was just a question of catching one more fish and salting him down for the winter. I asked him how he liked the reel — a borrowed one, costing $52.50. "It's all right," said Henry laconically and without enthusiasm. And then he added, with a proud shyness which I liked: "I bought a reel myself this spring. Paid five dollars for it. I can take it apart with my jackknife and fix the drag just to suit me. For *fishing*, it's just as good as that fifty-two-dollar one."

"For *fishing!*" Is not that, after all, the test? I am not foolish enough to believe that it is the country boy's traditional cut pole and bent pin that give him the advantage over the "city fellow" on a trout brook. His advantage does not lie in inferiority of apparent equipment, but in superiority of real equipment — in which tackle is only a minor element. If the Lord made that country boy a fisherman to begin with, and he knows the brook, he has already won more than half the battle. A good marksman with a poor rifle can outshoot a poor marksman with a good rifle. I reckon that superior excellence of tackle makes about ten per cent of one's fortune in fishing. Now a thrifty angler will not readily surrender that ten per cent of advantage. Chill penury should not repress his noble rage for the best outfit he can afford, even though he be, in Donald's phrase, "too poor to make the first payment on a fishhook." It is silly for him to mar his pleasure and his chances by using a reel that is liable to skip or bind or backlash, at precisely the wrong moment. But the point is that if your rod is supple enough to put out the line easily, and strong enough to hold your fish, you had better forget who built it and how much you paid for it, and concentrate your attention upon the far more important ninety per cent of the business, which depends not upon your outfit but upon yourself.

REVISITING A RIVER

I fished a certain pool in Nova Scotia once with three New Yorkers. Our tackle was costly and correct, and we had all had a fair amount of experience. We never raised a fish. Just as we were moving upstream a lady appeared upon the bank, followed by a slouching fellow carrying a gaff. She wore a black hat with a red feather, a dark skirt that came to her ankles, and she looked oddly out of place upon a salmon river. But she produced a light green-heart rod of native manufacture, spliced with electric tape, selected a fly from a small brown pasteboard box, and made a side-arm cast or two, to work her line out, which opened my eyes a little. And they were opened still wider when the lady tranquilly proceeded to hook and bring to the gaff two very fine salmon. Now I do not affirm that she killed those fish because she used an old-fashioned spliced rod. If she had traded rods with one of us she might have had even greater success. But her intangible equipment "for *fishing*" was infinitely better than ours. (I learned later that she lived on the first farm above the pool.)

In short, one must know a hundred things which are not set down in the Hardy or Mills catalogues of tackle, and which cannot be passed over the counter by the smoothest salesman that ever outfitted a green millionaire. Here, at this moment, is an illustration. Fifty yards in front of that cabin porch where we have been discussing theory and technique is the Cocktail Pool. Down toward the foot of it, by an egg-shaped blue rock that breaks the glassy current, I catch sight of the backfin and tail of a gently rising salmon. I pick up my rod and sneak down through the alders. My self-respect is beginning to return. In starting after that fish, inexpert as I am, I have one advantage over the most perfectly outfitted stranger, for I have fished that pool some hundreds of times and know precisely the distance for each cast and every trick of the current. Yet what I should like even better than hooking this particular salmon would be to know the answers to the unanswerable questions: Why is the salmon rising at this moment? Why should he rise again five minutes from now, as I trust he will, when the fly swings around the lower left-hand curve of that blue rock? Will it be a proof of hunger? Of curiosity? Of irritation? Of the play instinct? There are dozens of scientific chapters written on this topic, and no two of them agree. And why should he rise to-day to an artificial fly of one special color and pattern, and to no other, when none of the flies resemble closely any natural fly that can be seen in New Brunswick this month? And — apparently a far simpler question — why should salmon after salmon, in an endless procession, prefer the north side of that special blue rock? I took one there last night, and here is another! (I *lost him;* but we will forget that.)

Where the Clearwater joins the Miramichi, there is a flat white rock on the sandy bottom, so low and level that your eye cannot perceive that it gives any shelter;

and yet, for the last score of years, if there have been grilse in the river one has been lying beside that white rock. Two summers ago I watched for an hour a superb salmon under Ross's Bridge on the Margaree. A piece of white cardboard had blown off the bridge and sunk to the bottom, in about fifteen feet of water. That king salmon hovered just above it, moving twenty feet upstream at intervals of about two minutes, turning always at precisely the same point, like a restless tiger in a cage, and then drifting back downstream to his post above that sodden bit of paper. Was it a land-mark for him? Or was there a dead point in the current which had allowed the paper to sink, and which made it easier for the salmon to hover exactly there? We may have our guesses on all these matters, but we do not know. It is ninety years since the wisest of American writers gently reminded us that "we are as much strangers in Nature as we are aliens from God. We do not understand the notes of birds. The fox and the deer run away from us."

IV

Many nature-lovers are keenly conscious of the impression of changelessness, of timelessness, conveyed by any running stream. Carlyle writes of Annan Water in *Sartor:* "It struck me much, as I sat by the Kuhbach, one silent noontide, and watched it flowing, gurgling, to think how this same streamlet had flowed and gurgled, through all changes of weather and of fortune, from beyond the earliest date of History. Yes, probably on the morning when Joshua forded Jordan; even as at the midday when Cæsar, doubtless with difficulty, swam the Nile, yet kept his *Commentaries* dry, this little Kuhbach, assiduous as Tiber, Eurotas, or Siloa, was murmuring on across the wilderness, as yet unnamed, unseen."

One has this feeling often in the northern wilderness, where Indians are spearing and netting fish to-day from the same rocks on which Indians were standing when the canoes of the first *coureurs-de-bois* paddled up the St. Maurice or the Ottawa. Nothing seems to change, if you are only far enough north. The learned Cambridge chemists and physicists are now inclined to put the age of our planet — on the evidence furnished by the intricate and unhurried process by which Nature manufactures radium — at about 1,600,000,000 years. Reflecting on their calculations, last summer, and watching the huge glacial bowlder left stranded on the point near the head of Lake Nicotaus, I remarked to old John Sibley, the guide, "John, that rock has been there a long time." "Yes, sir," said John confidently, "I don't see that that rock has changed *any* in the fifty years that I've known it." If I had had a trained captive geologist in the canoe, he could have taught John that fifty years in the world of his science are less than a moment in the life of a lumberman.

Yet one of the discoveries that one makes in revisiting a river — even one whose banks and bed are largely worn out of the solid rock — is that the river is altering visibly from year to year. It is not the fact that we are now grown up which makes the old swimming hole of our boyhood days so strangely shallow. The truer explanation is that the hole has filled up with sand and gravel in the ceaseless process of erosion. On a swift river like the Miramichi there are ice jams and freshets to be reckoned with, to say nothing of the occasional dynamite used in the spring drive. "That pool has been no good since the freshet of 1923," say the guides, meaning that the rocks have been rolled down the ancient channels, filling in here and scooping out there, altering the currents, and disturbing, in some way we cannot fathom, the preferences of the fish. Five years, in fact, have made more changes in certain favorite pools of ours than I should have supposed were possible in five hundred. Some of the humble have been exalted and some of the mighty have been brought low. I confess that I have never noticed until this year, and then only when Donald pointed it out, that the big rocks which survive this age-long annual pressure of the ice jam are the ones whose upper surfaces slope upstream. The descending ice slides on up and over them, whereas a square rock which took the full force of that terrific impact would be torn from its bed. It is a curious instance of fitness for survival.

Even when your eye can detect no difference in the pool, the salmon find causes for dissatisfaction or for content. Sometimes, of course, you can reason the thing out, after a fashion: you can see that the colder water pouring in from Burnt Hill Brook, for instance, and traceable for two or three miles down the north shore of the river, has been diverted by some new heap of bowlders, so that the salmon in search of the "brook water" — which the guides distinguish sharply from what they call the "sour" river water — will now shelter themselves under a different ledge or hover in a deeper or shallower "run." Every trout fisherman knows that there are certain favorite places in a stream where the fish find the right food and shelter, and that these spots are moved into like the best rooms in a hotel. When one trout "checks out," either upstream or by capture, another promptly takes possession. Now a salmon, who almost certainly takes no food while in the river, — except perhaps the juice of some fly squeezed between his jaws and rapidly ejected, — chooses his temporary quarters in an apparently arbitrary fashion, with far less obvious attention to shelter than a trout. Many a skillful fly-caster who does not know these changes in the pools will be tempted to cast "over the fish's head" for a salmon that may be lying not fifteen feet away from him. In fact, anybody who has fished a strange salmon river alone, and then gone over the ground again with a competent guide, will admit his humiliation at having fished so stupidly at first, though his only real error lay in not knowing what it was impossible that he should know.

V

And no two summers are just alike. A year ago this week, according to C. E. B. C.'s log book, under precisely the same conditions as to weather and water, the Burnt

Hill salmon were rising plentifully to dry flies. This year they take the wet fly when they are taking anything. Last year there was only an average run of grilse; this year the river is full of them, and they are bigger and stouter in battle than for a score of years. What happened to them out in the mysterious Atlantic? Anglers will always have their moments of glory and their hours, or it may be whole days, of shame, but the moods of one visit to a river can never be repeated in the next. I am not sure, however, that the pleasures of recognition are not as deep as the joys of discovery. One remembers exactly where a big fish rose, — it may be five years ago or thirty, — and as you put your fly over what looks like the same ripple, you expect, in defiance of the laws of logic, that the miracle will happen again. And it often does — though this proves, perhaps, that fishing is an art and not a magic. An angler is bound to believe in the causes of effects. There was a reason for that fish's rising, once before, and now it is your privilege to

juggle with the causes until you can repro-
duce the effect. Yet what inconsistent rea-
soners we are! If the fish comes up in
accordance with your carefully worked-out
plan of campaign, it seems a triumphant
demonstration of the beneficent laws of the
universe. If he does n't rise, how easy it is
to slip back into the psychology of the
gambler or the medicine man, and to content yourself with phrases about luck! Or
you may turn materialist, blaming the wind
or the light or the barometer, or settle
down into the hopeless fatalism of declaring
that they are not "taking" to-day.

When this last mood is on you, the
remedy is to say casually to the head guide,
"Donald, it's fifty cents to a dime that *you*
can't raise a salmon." The Scotchman is
game. He borrows your rod, glances
through your disorderly fly book, selects
a fly as different as possible from the one
you have been using, and in a minute he is
at it, with that inimitable coaxing, wheed-
ling, teasing cast, very light and not too
long, covering each yard of water once and

once only, until suddenly there is a flash, an oath, — "*Holy Lazarus!*" — and before your duller senses have registered either the flash or the oath, Donald has struck him! Donald will lose that half dollar playing "forty-five" with the other guides to-night, but what of it? He has cured your fatalism.

I missed old John S. on the river this year. He must be nearly eighty, and, being a notoriously reckless and shiftless guide, I suspect that no one engaged him and that he was forced to stay in the settlements. But I could have put up with his poor cooking for the sake of seeing again his unique method of fly-casting. As he starts his backcast, he inhales a long rapt breath as if he were going into a trance, lifting his ribs and his elbows very high, like some strange old bird about to take flight. As the cast starts forward, he seems to breathe it out softly across the river, as gently as a child blowing dandelion seed. He gets an incredible distance, but I never saw him raise a fish.

Yet the story of John S.'s salmon at the

mouth of the Clearwater deserves to be set down. Improvident as ever, he was fishing with a frayed leader and with the one fly he owned, when he hooked and lost a big salmon — the leader parting. John was cast down but not destroyed. In his hat was a rusty long-shanked pickerel hook, and in the sandbank above the pool was the hole of a kingfisher. John puts in his hand cautiously and captures the mother bird on her nest, pulls out two or three feathers, — taking pains, he says, to hurt her feelings as little as possible, and replacing her gently on the eggs, — ties those feathers on the pickerel hook in imitation of a big Blue Doctor, and at the third cast he hooks and lands the identical runaway salmon, with the other fly and the broken leader still in its mouth! Whether there were reliable witnesses to this exploit I cannot say, but the sandbank is still there, and on the thirtieth of July, 1926, there was a hole in it which strongly suggested a kingfisher.

I miss also, this year, the companionship of a painter with whom I have fished many a stream, and whose eye was far quicker than mine in noting the changing colors of the water. There are no clay banks here, or rich alluvial meadows to help stain the river ten minutes after a shower. The Miramichi alters little at first, except to turn a slightly darker brown, while the bubbles and raindrops spoil its transparency. But as the rain comes more heavily, and the Burnt Hill Brook and the Clearwater begin to pour their brighter torrents into the main river, you can distinguish the brook water for a long distance on the north bank, and on the spring drive, I am told, the river men can trace it for a dozen miles — only they do not have, like my painter friend, a color vocabulary, any more than trout or salmon.

How under-vocabularied are most fishermen, likewise, in recording the charm of the changing sounds as the river falls or rises! When it is "holding," it seems hushed at noon, louder at dusk, and lower at dawn, but I am not sure. Certainly it grows hoarser and deeper with rising water until the flood covers most of the bowlders, and then it seems strangely quieter, except for the dull crumbling reverberation of the loose rocks as they are rolled along the deep-worn channels. I wish that Thoreau, whose ear was so acute for any sound in the woods, and whose "tree fall" sentence in the *Maine Woods* volume is one of the most perfect things in literature, had spent more time on big rocky rivers and less on the quiet, brimming Concord streams. He could have detected tones and overtones that are too subtle for my ear to catch distinctly. But what happiness, even for a dullard, to wake at night in your tent on the bluff above the rapids, and guess by the sound whether the river is rising or falling, or — by the sound again — whether the next day will be muggy or crystal clear!

VI

The guides, naturally, are far more weatherwise than we. They accept philosophically the long days of waiting for the river to come up or go down sufficiently to

give us the best fishing, for they are paid
by the day and the work here is light.
But they are as eager as we for a success-
ful trip, and they like a cold night or a
strong wind to stir up the fish and set
them traveling; and they hate as much as
we the ghastliness of very low water,
where all the bones of the starved stream
stick out, and you can scan the northwest
in vain for thunderheads. To these guides,
infinitely more than to any transient sportsman, the river is a living, sentient creature.
It is to them what Mother Earth was to
the Greeks. They were born on the river
and they will die on it, like their fathers.
They draw all their livelihood from it and
from the forests to which it is the only
path. Highlanders by race, and settled
here since their ancestors drove out the
French in the old wars, they keep alive
the history and romance of the river by
oral tradition. Nothing is lost, and it may
be that here and there the Celtic imagina-
tion adds something.

What talk I have heard, in low tones,

as the camp fire burns out and the fog rises ghostlike along the river! Not that these Scotchmen believe in ghosts; but they do believe in "forerunners." Were not three of them playing cards one night in our cabin, when they heard Sandy W.'s step on the west end of the porch? The step neared the door, and paused. "Hullo, Sandy," said the guides, scarcely looking up from the cards. Then they dropped the cards. *There was no one on the porch at all.* And Sandy W. had died that night, in Boston. That was a forerunner. And how about the fellow that owned the old camp by the spring opposite the mouth of the Clearwater? Two guides camping at the outlet, one autumn night, heard him call: "I want to come over!" They poled across in their log canoes, and as they poled he called again: "I want to come over!" But there was nobody in the old camp, and the owner, as they learned a month later, was five hundred miles away that night, crossing a far darker and deeper river than the Miramichi! The cry they heard was a forerunner.

Did not Donald himself, a Scotchman with nerve enough to stay alone one winter as watchman of the now abandoned tungsten mine, across the river from our camp, hear, late one afternoon, a call for "Help!" in the woods above the mine? It was thirty below zero, but he put on his snowshoes and climbed the hill, followed by his black cat. And there was just nothing; but as he neared the mine on his way back he heard that despairing cry once more. This time he stopped to make himself a cup of tea, and then took his rifle. And again there was nothing on the hilltop. But Donald did not sleep that night, and the next morning he tramped out to Maple Grove, to find that a friend of his had frozen to death the evening before, on top of his load of logs, some twenty miles from the mine. Now no man's voice can be heard for twenty miles, even in the silence of the winter woods. Donald knows that well enough; what he heard was a forerunner.

Have you ever heard of a "blood stopper"? There are ghastly injuries every season in the logging camps, even among this race of skilled axemen, and the surgery is rude. When a man is bleeding to death, the only hope lies in the services of a blood stopper — a man who possesses the mysterious power of causing the flow of blood to cease. The secret of this power can be passed on from a man to a woman or from a woman to a man, but — as I understand it — only one person in a family can exercise it in any generation. He must be brought as near as possible to the wounded man, must whisper the charmed syllables, — I was told with awe that they were "Bible words," — and then the blood instantly stops flowing. Only, mind you, if there is *any running water* between the blood stopper and the wounded man, the charm fails. Not until the hastily summoned blood stopper has crossed the last river or the last brook that lies between him and the sufferer does his magic gift prevail. What potency of evil, what enmity of healing power, can there be in a running stream? I do not know. But I have seen a blood stopper and a man

saved by him from death on last spring's
drive — unless these Scotchmen are in error.
Around the camp fire it is easier than elsewhere to indulge in that "willing suspension
of disbelief for the moment, which consti-
tutes poetic faith."

The truth is that to these men of the
Miramichi the love of the river and the
fear of the river, the history and romance
and superstition and toil and tragedy of
the river, are blended inextricably. Their
stories of Dead Man's Brook and of the
Island Mystery, of treasure buried by flee-
ing Frenchmen nearly two hundred years
ago and dug for at intervals ever since,
their memories of cold and hunger, of
poaching and fighting and triumphant hunting, pass into the blood of the listener.
Five years ago, a few hundred yards up
Burnt Hill Brook, I saw a paddle nailed
crosswise to a tree. On it was scribbled the
name of a young Frenchman, drowned
there on the spring drive, with the date.
This summer both name and date have
been washed out by the rain, but no human

hand will ever touch that rude cross, and no Miramichi man forgets it. Life on the river shares in the immense dignity of Death.

VII

Let us come back to our fishing. Among all these constant reminders of our ignorance, these equally constant but tiny accretions to our knowledge of the woods and the river, there are strange flashes of self-knowledge, too. Perhaps it is the sort of revelation for which hermits once tarried long in waste and solitary places. You come back to yourself. Companionship in the woods is essential if one is to keep his sanity, but a few hours of absolute solitude make for sanity also. Here you are, the same person that fished here five years or a score of years before, with the same slender collection of virtues, possibly, but certainly with the same large assortment of faults. Are you cursed with impatience, indecision, pedantry, envy, covetousness, and idolatry? An evening's fishing will

betray you as remorselessly as the Day of
Judgment.

I confess to wonderment and irritation
over the fisherman — though there are
legions of his type — who is always certain
that he has done the right thing in the
right way. If he loses a fish, it is demon-
strably the fault of the fish or of the reel
or of the fast water or of the guide who
was too slow with the gaff. I like much
better the lad who asks, "Dad, did I strike
that laker too quick, or was I too slow?"
Note that he does not blame either the fish
or the tackle, but only himself! And we
debate the question hour after hour, while
the boat swings at anchor on our little
Vermont lake and we wait for another
strike. Neither of us knows the right answer, and both of us are entirely happy,
having inherited an inquiring strain of
blood, some ability for seeing both sides of
a question, and a deep respect for "hunches."

It was a fisherman on our lake, by the
way, who once gave me a thoroughly local
interpretation of the story of the Miracu-

lous Draught of Fishes. In this lake the biggest trout lie in pockets along the edge of the ledges, sixty or seventy feet down, and it takes a good eye for landmarks to anchor the boat precisely in the right spot. Often one side of the boat, when two men are fishing, will have all the luck, that four or five feet of difference in latitude or longitude meaning success or failure in reaching the big lakers with your minnow. Hence my old friend's cautious and entirely reverent attempt at New Testament exegesis: "Mr. Perry, don't you think that when our Lord told the disciples to let down the net on the other side of the boat, *He had a hunch that they was anchored just on the aidge of a laidge?*"

I cannot say that there was anything miraculous about our draught of fishes on the Miramichi this summer, unless it be in the number and size and splendid fighting quality of the grilse. The salmon fishing was below the average. But somehow the great pork barrel on the east porch of the cabin kept filling steadily with salted fish —

and by and by we began to feel the premonitions of departure. Ominous yellow leaves appear on the tips of the young white birches across the river. We have no other calendar with us than such signs of the passing weeks and a hint from the cook that we must hold back a little on this or that delicacy. I notice that G., who expects some trout-fishing elsewhere in August, begins to talk about the fun of dry-fly fishing with your very lightest tackle on some brimming meadow brook where there would be no danger of a rushing grilse or salmon wrecking your rod. Alas for the inconsistency of fishermen! We hook and release every day, here on the river, trout that would astonish our friends at home, and already, with shoulder blades still aching with swinging a salmon rod, we are dreaming of meadow brooks in New England. And nothing is more certain than that when we are floating our tiniest flies again over one of those brooks we shall dream of the sudden sullen plunge of a salmon!

The final morning comes, and that "one

more" cast which every angler knows. For me it is always an excessively solemn rite and is usually unattended with any luck whatever. But on this occasion, as I was slowly reeling in, a besotted salmon, hovering in the ripple not six yards below me, seemed to decide from the melancholy look upon my face that it was now or never! I struck, for once, just as he flashed, and he was so well hooked that even I could not have lost him. He weighed only ten pounds, but I am sure that he possessed a most magnanimous soul.

Reluctantly we settled ourselves into the canoes at last, at the head of the Pond, bound homeward. As I took a final look at the rough water between my canoe and the ledge on the opposite shore, a huge salmon leaped, as if with an ironic gesture of farewell. He looked exactly like the monster that had carried off my Dusty Miller and a bit of broken leader, in that very spot, ten days before. Well, I hope now that he will rub that fly off upon the rocks long before the spawning season! I had hated to lose him, but I cannot help admiring, this morning, that sardonic parting assertion of superiority. "Canst thou draw out leviathan with an hook?" he seems to shout as he plunges down, while the river, for a moment, seems strangely flat and empty.

"Perhaps not, old fellow," I whisper to him, as I pick up the bow paddle instead of a rod and we head downstream. "Perhaps not, but there is another summer coming! Au revoir! May no poacher's net entangle you or otter tear you. May you not linger under the river ice all winter and become a mere 'black salmon,' to rise hungrily in the broad eddies at any lure next spring. May you rather go down proudly into the North Atlantic and take your lordly ease in the great deep until some full tide next June. Then may you make gallantly the long uphill climb against one hundred and thirty miles of tumbling water, and settle again in the old pool under the gray ledge. And if in some soft July twilight you swirl up once more at a Dusty Miller or a Silver Doctor, may it be a fair fight, and may the leader hold!"